Fish

Sally Morgan

Raintree

Chicago, Illinois

For information, address the publisher:
Raintree, 100 N. LaSalle, Suite 1200, Chicago, IL 60602

Produced for Raintree by
White-Thomson Publishing Ltd.

Consultant: Dr. Rod Preston-Mafham
Page layout by Tim Mayer
Photo research by Sally Morgan

Originated by Dot Gradations Ltd.
Printed in China by WKT Company Limited

09 08 07 06 05
10 9 8 7 6 5 4 3 2 1

Library of Congress Cataloging-in-Publication Data
Morgan, Sally.
  Fish / Sally Morgan.
    p. cm. -- (Animal kingdom)
  Includes bibliographical references (p.   ).
  Contents: Fish -- Swimming -- Fish senses -- Jawless fish -- Sharks as hunters -- Eels -- Salmon.
  ISBN 1-4109-1048-2 (lib. bdg.) -- ISBN 1-4109-1345-7 (pbk.)
  1. Fishes--Juvenile literature. [1. Fishes.] I. Title. II.
Series: Animal kingdom (Chicago, Ill.)
  QL617.2.M67 2004
  597--dc22

                                  2003026279

Acknowledgments
The publisher would like to thank the following for permission to reproduce copyright materials: Corbis **Title page,** pp.**4, 6** bottom, **11** bottom, **13** bottom, **18** bottom, **21** top and bottom (Brandon Cole), **22, 16, 28–29, 32, 33** bottom, **35** top, **39** bottom, **51** top, **53** top, **59, 60, 61**; Ecoscene pp.**5** top (John Liddiard), **6** top (Jeff Collett), **9** top (Chinch Gryniewicz), **9** bottom (John Lewis), **10** (John Liddiard), **15** bottom (Kjell Sandved), **18** top (Phillip Colla), **19** (Reinhard Dirscherl), **24** top, **25, 27** top and bottom, **29, 31** top, (Phillip Colla), **33** top (Jeff Collett), **45** bottom and **48** (Reinhard Dirscherl), **49** top (John Lewis), **50, 51** bottom (Reinhard Dirscherl), **52** (John Lewis), **53** bottom (Alan Towse), **55** top (Quentin Bates), **55** bottom (Martha Collard), **57** bottom (Jeff Collett); Ecoscene / V&W pp.**11** top, **45** top, **46–47, 54, 58** (Brandon Cole); Ecoscene/Papilio pp.**13** top (Peter Tatton), **15** top (Clive Druett), **30** top (Steve Jones), **36** (Robert Pickett); Getty Images p.**56**; Nature Picture Library pp.**14** (Hermann Brehm), **16–17** (David Shale), **20** (Reijo Juurinen), **28** top (Jeff Rottman), **30–31**(Georgette Douwma), **43** top (Jurgen Freund); NHPA pp.**5** bottom, **7** (Steve Dalton), **8** (Lutra), **12** (Pete Atkinson), **23** top (Linda Pitkin), **23** bottom, **24** bottom, **34** (ANT), **35** bottom, **37** top (Daniel Heuclin), **37** bottom (Kevin Schafer), **38** (Lutra), **39** top, **40** (Norbert Wu), **41** top (Roger Tidman), **41** bottom (Norbert Wu), **42** (Lutra), **43** bottom (Ernie Janes), **44** (Kevin Schafer), **57** top (Martin Patrick O'Neill).

Front cover photograph of blue-lined snappers reproduced with permission of NHPA (B. Jones and M. Shimlock). Back cover photograph of a trigger fish reproduced with permission of Corbis.

Every effort has been made to contact copyright holders of any material reproduced in this book. Any omissions will be rectified in subsequent printings if notice is given to the publisher.

Contents

Introducing Fish

Fish are aquatic animals. This means that they live in water. Fish are found living in virtually every watery habitat on Earth. From the deepest ocean trenches to the highest alpine lakes and underground caves, wherever there is permanent water, you will probably find fish. There are more than 27,500 species of fish.

Vertebrates

Fish belong to a large group of animals called vertebrates. These are animals with backbones. The backbone is like a stiff rod with a bundle of nerves called the spinal cord running through the middle. Other vertebrates include amphibians, reptiles, birds, and mammals.

Classification

Living organisms are classified, or organized, according to how closely related one organism is to another. The basic group in classification is the species. For example, human beings belong to the species *Homo sapiens*. A species is a group of individuals that are similar to each other and that can interbreed with one another. Species are grouped together into genera (singular: genus). A genus may contain a number of species that share some features. *Homo* is the human genus. Genera are grouped together in families, families grouped into orders, and orders are grouped into classes. Classes are grouped together in phyla (singular: phylum) and, finally, the phyla are grouped into kingdoms. Kingdoms are the largest groups. Fish belong to the animal kingdom.

▶ This tiny fringehead is small enough to hide in holes where it is safe from predators.

Fins

Fish are vertebrates that do not have limbs. They have fins instead. The fin of a bony fish consists of a thin flap of skin supported by very thin, long bones called spines. Some of the fins are arranged in pairs and stick out from the sides of the body. These are called paired fins. They include the pectoral fins located behind the head and the pelvic fins that lie further back. The pectoral fins are the equivalent to arms in a human being while the pelvic fins are the equivalent to legs. The other single fins include the dorsal, ventral, and tail fins.

Classification key

KINGDOM	Animalia
PHYLUM	Chordata
SUBPHYLUM	Vertebrata
CLASSES	5
ORDERS	62
SPECIES	approximately 27,500

dorsal fin

tail fin

pectoral fin

ventral fin

pelvic fin

▼ The archerfish knocks small insects off leaves and into the water by firing a jet of water at them.

▲ Fish share many similar characteristics. This colorful garibaldi is a bony fish found off the coast of California.

Five classes

Fish differ from the other vertebrates because they are not grouped into a single class, but rather into five related classes. These are the jawless fish (Myxini and Cephalaspidomorphi), the cartilaginous fish (Chondrichthyes), and the bony fish (Sarcopterygii and Actinopterygii). Bony fish represent 95 percent of all fish.

Fish have adapted to living in water. A fish has fins rather than limbs and gills instead of lungs. Gills are found behind the head on either side of the body. They look a bit like the rounded ends of feathers. They are red because they are filled with blood. Bony fish have four gills on either side of the head, each supported by a curved bar made of cartilage. In human beings, cartilage is the flexible material found in our noses and ears. Water enters the fish through the mouth, passes between and over the gills, and leaves through the gill cover, or operculum. The oxygen in the water is picked up by blood as it passes through the gills, allowing the fish to breathe.

▲ In many fish, the gills are protected by a movable bony flap called the *operculum*.

Ectothermic animals

Fish are described as ectothermic, or cold-blooded. This means that the body temperature of a fish matches the temperature of the water around it. The temperature of large bodies of water, such as the ocean, does not vary greatly, so most fish do not have to cope with a broad range of temperatures.

▼ The squirrel fish is nocturnal, feeding at night and using its large eyes to spot prey.

Movement

A fish moves through water by swimming. Its body shape has adapted to make this as efficient as possible. Most fish have streamlined, or torpedo-shaped, bodies. This shape reaches a maximum width about a third of the way back and then gradually tapers towards the tail, allowing the fish to slip smoothly through the water. The skin is often covered with overlapping scales. Scales protect the fish and prevent water from passing through its skin. Most bony fish have an outer covering of mucus that makes them slippery and may prevent parasites from attaching to them.

Amazing facts

- The ice fish of the freezing Antarctic waters has a kind of antifreeze in its cells to prevent it from freezing solid.
- The age of a bony fish can be determined by counting the number of rings on its scales.
- The mudskipper has pectoral fins that look like little legs. It uses these supports to walk from pool to pool.

Swim bladder

Bony fish have a swim bladder, a bag of air like a balloon, just below the backbone. This helps to keep the fish floating at the right depth in the water. Fish can adjust the amount of air in the swim bladder. By adding more air to the swim bladder, the fish becomes more buoyant and rises toward the surface. If there is less air in the swim bladder, the fish sinks lower. Cartilaginous fish rely on their large fins and a fatty liver for lift. The liver contains oil that is lighter than water and gives buoyancy. When the fish stops swimming, it sinks to the seabed.

▲ At low tide, the mudskipper uses its fleshy pectoral fins to move over mud.

Life Cycle of a Fish

Most fish lay eggs that hatch into larvae. However, some species of sharks and rays keep their eggs within the body and give birth to live young.

Laying eggs

Bony fish use external fertilization. This means that the female lays her eggs in water and they are fertilized afterwards by the male. Each egg contains a larval fish. Some eggs contain oil that makes them float, while others have a sticky covering so they attach to objects in the water. The eggs hatch, and the young larvae emerge. The larval fish has a yolk sac full of food. This feeds the larva for the first few weeks of life. Over time the larvae grow larger and begin to look more like adults. In some species, such as salmon, this can take several years.

Some eggs are simple, rounded structures that contain the larva, a yolk sac, and little else. Some sharks produce a small number of eggs, each contained within a large, leathery case. There is a large yolk sac inside. Sharks do not have a free-swimming larval stage.

◄ Larval trout, called fry, hatch from an egg with a yolk sac attached to their bodies.

Live young

Some larger species of sharks and rays are viviparous, which means they give birth to live young. The female keeps the eggs inside her body. The larvae hatch inside her body and she gives birth to them. In a few sharks, such as the lemon and blue sharks, there is a connection between the mother and the larvae, and food is passed along it. Once the young sharks are born, they swim away from their mothers.

▲ The egg of the dogfish is large and leathery. Spiral threads attach it to rocks and seaweed so it does not float away.

Parental care

Most bony fish lay their eggs and forget about them. The female fish lays many thousands, sometimes millions, of eggs so that a few may survive to become adults. However, some species, such as sea horses and cichlids, look after their eggs. They keep their eggs clean and free from disease and guard them from predators. Some make a nest for their eggs. They may care for their young after they hatch, too. This means that more of the young fish survive to adulthood.

Amazing facts

- When a type of cichlid called a mouthbreeder has laid her eggs, she keeps them in her mouth until they hatch.
- Baby gray nurse sharks often eat each other while inside their mother. Larger ones eat smaller ones so only one or two are born.
- The female sea horse places her eggs in the male's pouch, where they hatch. The young are released up to six weeks later.

► This pair of sea horses have used their tails to attach themselves to some seaweed. The pouch of the male sea horse, on the right, is swollen with eggs.

Swimming

All fish can swim, but some swim much more quickly than others. The fastest-swimming fish have torpedo-shaped bodies, while those that live on reefs tend to have shorter bodies that are flattened vertically. They have less need for speed but must be able to dart between the rocks to find food and escape from predators.

How fish swim

Most fish swim by alternately tightening and relaxing the muscles on either side of the body. This bends the body from side to side. Fish can do this because they have a flexible backbone. The tail fin pushes against the water. This action propels the fish forward in the same way that oars propel a rowing boat. Eels and other snakelike fish swim by pushing themselves in a wavelike motion through the water. This movement, which is similar to that of a snake moving on land, is a relatively slow movement and uses up a lot of energy.

▼ Sharks have streamlined bodies with powerful tails and long tail fins that push them through the water.

▲ The dorsal and ventral fins prevent this queen angelfish from rolling from side to side.

▲ Butterfly fish have bodies that are flattened from the sides. They use paired fins to steer around rocks on coral reefs.

Balance

The tail fin is not the only fin a fish uses to swim. A fish needs to balance its body in the water and steer. The single dorsal and ventral fins prevent the fish from rolling from side to side. These fins also stop yawing. Yawing occurs when the tail pushes to one side, causing the head to swing, too. The fins reduce the distance the fish's head can move. The paired fins control the up and down movements. By altering the angle of these fins, the fish can swim up or down in the water. The dorsal and ventral fins are also used to help the fish stay in one place and even move backward.

Braking

Paired fins are also used as brakes and for steering. This is very useful to fish such as butterfly fish or damsel fish. They live along rocky shores or coral reefs where they may chase prey around corners or make short, sharp turns to escape from a predator. Some fish, such as puffers, trunkfish, and rays, use only their pectoral fins for swimming.

Amazing facts

- The fastest shark is the short fin mako (*Isurus oxyrinchus*). It can reach swimming speeds of up to 20 miles (32 kilometers) per hour.
- The huge wings of rays and skates are actually pectoral fins.
- Tuna undertake some of the longest migrations of any fish. During the 1950s, a tagged tuna was caught after swimming from Mexico to Japan, a distance of more

Ocean Hunters

The most advanced swimmers are the predators of the open ocean. They include marlin, tuna, and the mackerel sharks, such as mako sharks and great whites. These fish have the ultimate in streamlined bodies. They are long, torpedo-shaped, and covered by smooth skin. The tail is narrow and sickle-shaped to produce maximum power with minimum effort.

These predators have thin, stiff fins they can fold back into slots to increase the streamlining. The shape of the fins gives lift and flexibility, just like the wings of a bird in the air. In some fish, the fins can be flipped open like a fan when they want to stop. Some predator fish, such as swordfish, have upper jaws that are elongated into a spear. This maximizes the streamlining and acts as a powerful weapon.

▲ One of the most feared fish in the ocean is the shark. It is known for its wide mouth and well-developed senses.

Amazing facts

- Predatory fish, such as sharks, have such well-developed senses that they can hunt day or night and chase prey into the dark ocean depths.
- The sailfish reaches speeds of more than 68 miles (110 kilometers) per hour.
- The salmon shark can maintain its body temperature at 77 °F (25 °C). That is about 70 °F (21 °C) above the temperature of the subarctic waters where it lives.

▲ Barracudas, which hunt in large schools, are dangerous predators. They have a particularly large lower jaw and extremely sharp teeth.

Trapping prey

These fish may swim thousands of miles across the oceans in search of food. They have to be efficient so that they do not use too much energy. Predator fish need enough energy left to shoot through the water and run down their prey. Often these predators work together to surround a school of fish such as herring or mackerel, taking turns to swim into the shoal and catch fish.

Warm muscles

Fish are ectothermic, but many predators have to dive into deep, cold water to catch prey. They need warm muscles to be able to swim efficiently. Otherwise, the chilly waters would slow them down. Muscles release heat when they are used, so these predatory fish have blood vessels that run close to the blocks of muscles. The blood gets warmed as it passes near the muscles. The warm blood circulates around the body, allowing the fish to stay alert and active for much longer.

▲ Sharks, such as this blue shark, may swim through a school of fish to break it up. This makes it easier to catch an individual fish.

13

Fish Senses

Living in water is very different from living on land. Land animals rely heavily on their sight, but in water, sight is less useful because the water may be very murky. Fish rely more on their senses of smell, hearing, and taste, as well as the ability to detect vibrations.

Fish eyes are adapted to seeing under water. Many species can see in murky water and can see in color. Fish have nostrils that they use to detect smell. In some fish, such as eels and salmon, this sense is particularly good. They can distinguish between the waters of different rivers in order to identify their home river. Predatory fish can detect the scents of mucus, droppings, and other debris left in the water by their prey.

Fish have ears inside their skulls. They can detect sound waves that travel from the water through the bones of the skull to the ear. Detecting sound is particularly important at night when sight is of little use. Many fish hide during the day and come out to feed only at night, when predators are less likely to spot them. They use sound to communicate with each other. Some fish also have taste buds in their mouth, on their skin, and on their fins.

▼ The electric eel lives in murky water and navigates by using electrical signals.

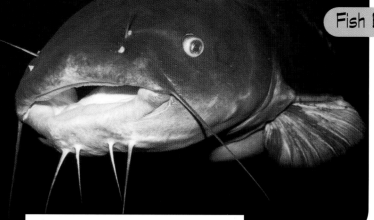

▲ Catfish have whiskerlike barbels around the mouth. The barbels are covered in taste buds and are used to find food.

Lateral line

Running along each side of a fish's body is the lateral line, a long canal that lies just beneath the surface of the skin. Pores at regular intervals connect the canal to the surface. Sensory cells within the canal can detect the slightest vibration in the water. This enables schooling fish to stay together, predatory fish to detect their prey, and smaller fish to avoid their enemies.

Amazing facts

- Sound travels five times faster through water than it does in air.
- The Japanese weatherfish gets its name because it is sensitive to changes in atmospheric pressure. It is most active when pressure is low and when the weather is changing.
- The blind cave fish finds its food using smell and navigates using its well-developed lateral line.

Electrical signals

Sharks and rays have another sensory system, called the ampullae of Lorenzini, that detects electrical signals produced by the muscle movements of their prey. Some fish, such as the knife fish and the elephant nose fish, can produce electricity as well as detect electrical signals. They use this ability as a radar system to find their way around muddy waters and to detect prey. The fish emits a series of electrical signals that get distorted by objects, providing the fish with a kind of map of its surroundings.

◄ The blind cave fish lives in caves where it is too dark to see. It has no eyes and relies on its other senses to navigate.

Deep-sea Fish

▲ The aristostomias has a number of light-producing organs. One can be seen here, just below its eye.

Fish that live in the deepest parts of the ocean are very different from surface-swimming fish. They are adapted to life in cold, dark water. At depth, the weight of the water pushes down, creating a high pressure. The bodies of all deep-water inhabitants are adapted to survive these high pressures.

Life in the twilight zone

The twilight zone is between 200 and 1000 meters below sea level. Good eyesight is important, so fish that live in the twilight zone have large eyes. Many have eyes that can look up toward the light so they can spot the silhouette of prey above them. Many deep-sea fish are camouflaged so predators do not see them. Some have completely transparent bodies that make them seem invisible. Others have silver sides that act like mirrors to reflect any light away so they can move unseen.

▲ The winteria has two large eyes that point upward to spot the silhouettes of prey above.

Amazing facts

- The loose-jawed dragon fish produces red light from an organ behind its head. It may use this to find its prey.
- The fertilized eggs of the anglerfish float to the surface of the water, where the larvae hatch. When the young fish are large enough, they sink back down to the deep.
- The greatest depth at which a fish has been caught is 27,454 feet (8,368 meters).

Making light

Beneath the twilight zone, it is completely dark, and there is no need for camouflage. A few fish can even make their own light. This is called bioluminescence. Their special light-producing organs can be switched on and off. Some fish use the light to attract prey, while others use it to attract mates.

Little food

The biggest problem facing animals of the deep is the severe lack of food. The fish have to survive on what little floats down from above, or feed on the other deep-sea fish. They cannot waste energy by swimming around looking for food. Many lie motionless in the water and wait for prey to swim past. They are sensitive to the tiniest vibrations that may be created by their prey. These fish often have sharp teeth, big mouths and flexible stomachs to catch prey and swallow it whole. Deep-sea fish grow very slowly and most are small. This is due to the cold and the lack of food.

▼ The anglerfish has a thin, pointed fin that hangs above its mouth like a fishing rod. This acts as a lure to attract prey. The anglerfish snaps them up in its massive mouth.

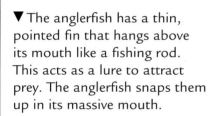

Fish Classes

Scientists believe that fish were the first animals to have a true backbone. Although all fish have fins and use gills, they are not sorted into a single class. Instead, they are sorted into five classes: Myxini, Cephalaspidomorphi, Chondrichthyes, Sarcopterygii, and Actinopterygii. There is much debate concerning the classification of fish. Evidence from fish DNA suggests that some fish may need to be reclassified. This book uses the five-class system, but some biologists believe that the cartilaginous fish (Chondrichthyes) should be split into two separate classes.

▲ This stingray, with its flattened body and winglike fins, is a cartilaginous fish.

Within these five classes there are 62 different orders and at least 27,500 different species. Scientists are discovering more species all the time, so the numbers continue to increase. The fish are classified according to the type of material that makes up their skeleton, such as whether it is cartilaginous or bony. Some fish are classified by their lack of jaws. Each of these classes has evolved separately from one another.

Primitive jawless fish form the classes Myxini and Cephalaspidomorphi. However, most fish belong to the class of either cartilaginous fish or bony fish. Cartilaginous fish are divided into three smaller groups—sharks, rays, and chimaeras—according to their body shapes and the number of gill slits. Bony fish make up the bulk of all fish species.

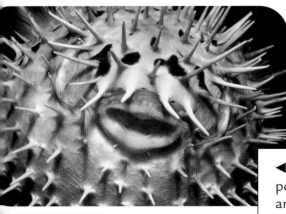

◄ It may not look much like a fish, but this is a porcupine fish. When threatened, it swallows water and inflates its body, causing its spines to stick out.

Early fish

The first fish appeared about 500 million years ago. These early fish were similar to the jawless fish that exist today. Fish with jaws did not appear for another 50 to 60 million years. An important group of ancestral fish were the acanthodians, or spiny sharks. Unlike the jawless fish, these fish had teeth so they could feed on a wide range of foods. Their name, spiny shark, comes from the pairs of spines that stuck out of the lower body. It is thought that paired fins evolved from these spines. Scales covered the bodies of the fish. The ancestors of sharks and rays appeared before bony fish—approximately 370 million years ago.

Amazing facts

- The sawfish is named after its long, sawlike snout, which is up to 6.5 feet (2 meters) long and has between 24 and 32 pairs of teeth on either side.
- The flying fish, a type of bony fish, uses its paired fins to glide for up to 665 feet (200 meters) over the surface of the water to escape predators.

▼ These sweetlips are bony fish found in warm waters around coral reefs.

Jawless Fish

Jawless fish belong to a primitive class of fish. They were the earliest fish that first appeared about 500 million years ago. Most species are now extinct, but scavenging hagfish and blood-sucking lampreys still exist.

No jaw

The main feature of these fish is the complete lack of a jaw. The mouth is like a hole in the head. Lampreys have a sucker that surrounds the mouth. This sucker can be as wide as the animal's body and has a fringed edge. In the place of a jaw is a rough, tonguelike structure covered in many teeth. Jawless fish have a long, slimy eel-like body. There are no scales over the skin. These fish also lack the paired pelvic and pectoral fins seen in other fish, and they do not have a true backbone. The gill openings are small and rounded.

Classification key

CLASS	Myxini (hagfish) and Cephalaspidomorphi (lampreys)
ORDERS	2
FAMILIES	4
SPECIES	approximately 90

▼ A sea lamprey has a mouth surrounded by a sucker and seven round gill openings behind the head.

Amazing facts

- The hagfish is also called the slime eel because it secretes vast amounts of slime from pores along its sides.
- Young sea lampreys are blind and toothless. They take six years to become adults.
- Adult brook lampreys die after spawning.

▲ The hagfish does not have a jaw. It has small teeth that it uses to attach itself to its food.

Feeding

Most adult lampreys suck the blood of other fish. They are parasites because they attach to and harm another animal, called the host. The lamprey clings to the skin of its host using its sucker and teeth, and sucks the blood using a rough tongue. It stays attached to the host for many weeks until the host dies from loss of blood. Young lampreys feed on microscopic organisms in the water.

Hagfish feed on dead and decaying animals that have sunken to the seabed. Hagfish have a good sense of smell that they use to find food. The hagfish feeds by putting its head inside the body of a decaying animal and sucking the rotting flesh into its mouth. Its body is covered in a thick slime that makes it slippery. Predators cannot hold on to the incredibly slimy body!

Habitat and life cycle

Hagfish are found only in salt water. They lay large eggs in a tough, leathery case, and the young hagfish emerge looking like small adults. Sea lampreys live in salt water but return to freshwater to breed. They die after laying their eggs. Young lampreys go through several larval stages before they eventually return to the sea. Brook lampreys spend all of their lives in freshwater.

▲ Pores in the skin of the hagfish release large quantities of slime.

Cartilaginous Fish

Cartilaginous fish have skeletons made of cartilage rather than of bone. They are divided into two subclasses: ratfish and chimaeras (Holocephali), and the more varied Elasmobranchii, which includes sharks, skates, rays, and sawfish. Cartilage is much more flexible and far lighter than bone, and it is not strong enough to support the weight of a land animal. However, fish are supported by water, and so cartilage is strong enough to support some of the largest fish in the sea.

Other features of this group include an upper jaw that is not fused to the skull. Cartilaginous fish do not have swim bladders, but they do have an oily liver that provides lift.

▲ Rays, such as this southern stingray, have pectoral fins that look like wings.

Sandpaper skin

The skin of cartilaginous fish is unusual. The skin of a shark, for example, is rough and feels like sandpaper. It is made up of thousands of tiny, backward-pointing scales called dermal denticles that look like teeth.

▲ The dogfish is a small shark that hunts on the seabed in shallow water. Its coloring allows it to blend in with the seabed.

As the fish grows, the scales do not increase in size. Instead, the fish grows more scales. Some rays have large scales while chimaeras have very few or none at all. Cartilaginous fish have teeth formed from modified scales. Sharks and rays continually lose and replace their teeth throughout their lives.

Gill slits

Cartilaginous fish have internal gills. On the outside of the body is a series of gill slits. Rays and sharks have between five and seven pairs, while chimaeras have only one pair. When the mouth opens to let in water, the gill slits are closed. Then the mouth shuts and the water is forced between and over the gills, which absorb oxygen, and out through the gill slits.

Reproduction

Cartilaginous fish use internal fertilization. The eggs are fertilized by the male while they are still inside the female's body. Sharks produce eggs with leathery egg cases. Many lay egg cases filled with food for the embryo inside. Some female sharks keep the eggs within the body and give birth to live young.

▼ The elephant shark belongs to the suborder Holocephali because it only has one gill slit on each side of the head.

Sharks

Sharks belong to the group
of cartilaginous fish called
elasmobranchs. They have
streamlined bodies, powerful tails,
and paired, triangular fins. Sharks
swim slowly over long distances and are
found in all the oceans and at all depths.
The shark that lives at the greatest depth is
the rarely seen megamouth. Most sharks are solitary animals, though a few,
such as the spiny dogfish and hammerhead shark, form schools.

▲ The horn shark feeds mainly
on invertebrate animals found
on the seabed.

Dividing up the sharks

The sharks are subdivided into two groups, or superorders. The
superorder Squalea is comprised of the primitive six-gill sharks, deepwater
sharks, dogfish sharks, skates, and rays. The superorder Galeomorphii is
the larger of the groups, making up 75 percent of all sharks. Features that
help in the classification of sharks include the number of gill slits, the
presence of dorsal fin spines, an anal fin, and the position of the eye
relative to the mouth. Some sharks have a thin, tough inner eyelid, called
a nictitating membrane. This membrane covers the eye to protect it from
damage. This is especially important during an attack because a prey fish
might harm the shark as it struggles to escape.

▼ The largest shark is the whale
shark, with a length of 39 feet
(12 meters) and a weight of
more than 13 tons.

▲ This blue shark is looking for small fish beneath a floating mass of kelp.

Classification key

CLASS	Chondrichthyes
SUBCLASS	**Elasmobranchii**
SUPERORDERS	Squalea and Galeomorphii
ORDERS	8
FAMILIES	31
SPECIES	approximately 800

No swim bladder

Sharks do not have swim bladders. They rely on their fins to give them lift to rise up in the water or to sink, just as a plane gets lift from its wings. The liver of the shark is large and rich in oil, which gives the shark buoyancy. However, sharks have to swim all the time. When they stop swimming, they sink to the seabed.

Shark facts

- One of the smallest sharks is the deepwater dogfish shark, *Etmopterus perryi*. This species is found in the Caribbean Sea and is less than 8 inches (20 centimeters) long.

- The tiger shark is considered one of the most dangerous sharks because it is the most common large shark. It hunts in shallow waters and will eat anything that fits in its mouth!

Swim to breathe

Most sharks have to keep moving to breathe and stay alive. They breathe by swimming forward with their mouths open, allowing water to flow across their gills. Most cannot stop for long or move backward like the bony fish can. Sometimes sharks rest in places where there is a current so water moves over their gills.

25

▲ The great white shark often swims along with its teeth showing. The first two rows are used for grabbing and cutting up its prey.

Sharks as hunters

Most sharks are predators. They can swim at high speed over short distances to catch their prey in open water. They will also lie in wait for prey and catch it as it passes close by. However, some sharks are scavengers that feed on the dead bodies of other animals. Sharks have many ways of finding their prey. They can detect blood or dead remains in the water from a distance of several miles and can pick up the sounds of animals in the water. As they get closer they can feel vibrations in the water. Once they have almost reached their prey, sharks rely on their sight. In murky water, sharks can often see better than their prey can.

Electrical detection

Sharks and rays have a series of tiny gel-filled pits on their snouts called the ampullae of Lorenzini. These sensitive pits pick up weak electrical signals produced by muscle movements of animals.

◄ The tiny pits on the snout of this blue shark are the ampullae of Lorenzini.

In for the kill

The teeth of the larger sharks, such as the great white, are large and triangular, with jagged edges that are perfect for ripping into prey. When teeth are lost, they are quickly replaced. Rows of teeth continually form at the back of the mouth and gradually move forward toward the edge of the mouth. Not all predatory sharks have large teeth. For example, the horn shark has rows of tiny teeth that grow close together and form a rough plate for crushing small crustaceans such as prawns or crabs.

Sharks often circle their prey before making one last charge. Mako sharks approach their prey at great speed from below. They have dark upper bodies, and so cannot be seen easily by their prey against the dark water below. They have paler undersides to their bodies, which also makes them difficult to spot from below. This is called countershading.

Amazing facts

- The great white shark is responsible for more attacks on people than any other shark.
- Tiger sharks eat a great range of animals. In fact, they eat anything they can catch alive.
- Research has shown that sharks may be more than ten times as sensitive to light as people.

▼ This small horn shark is feeding on squid eggs on the seabed.

The Hammerhead Shark

The hammerhead shark gets its name from its strangely shaped head, which looks like a double-headed hammer. There are 8 hammerhead shark species. They range in size from just under 3 feet (1 meter) to around 20 feet (6 meters) long.

The hammer

The shark's eyes and nostrils are located at the extreme ends of the hammer structure, which is called a cephalophoil. It is thought that this unusual head structure may give the shark some sensory advantages. With an increased distance between the nostrils, hammerheads may be better able to track scent trails. The widely spaced eyes give hammerheads binocular vision. This allows the fish to create a three-dimensional image so it can judge distances more easily.

The cephalophoil may also help provide lift and maneuverability. All sharks have large pectoral fins to help buoyancy, but the hammerhead's cephalophoil may provide extra lift. Hammerheads have larger muscles in the head region compared with closely related sharks, and a wider range of head movement. This allows them to maneuver quickly at high speeds.

▲ The hammerhead shark's unusual head has eyes that are far apart. This may help the shark to judge distances.

Classification key

CLASS	Chondrichthyes
SUBCLASS	Elasmobranchii
ORDER	Carcharhiniformes
FAMILY	Carcharhinidae
GENUS	Sphyrna
SPECIES	**8, including *lewini* (the scalloped hammerhead) and *mokarran* (great hammerhead)**

▶ Large schools of scalloped hammerheads gather to breed. At night they split up to hunt for squid.

◀ Hammerhead sharks feed on a variety of animals, including fish and squid.

A fierce predator

The great hammerhead is a fierce predator with a good sense of smell that it uses to find prey. The teeth are triangular with extremely jagged edges. Hammerheads eat a range of prey such as bony fish, rays and other sharks, squid, octopuses, and crustaceans. Stingrays seem to be a particular favorite of the great hammerhead. The great hammerhead uses its cephalophoil to pin the stingray down while it takes bites from its wings. The great hammerhead has also been known to attack other hammerheads.

Live births

The hammerheads are viviparous, which means they give birth to live young. The great hammerhead produces up to 40 pups, each of which is about 27 inches (70 centimeters) long. The head of a newborn pup is more rounded than that of an adult, but this changes as it grows.

Amazing facts

- Great hammerheads commonly prey on stingrays. One shark was found with 96 poisonous stingray barbs embedded in its mouth and jaws.
- The largest reported great hammerhead shark was 20 feet (6 meters) long. Hammerheads can weigh as much as 1,00 pounds (450 kilograms).
- Smooth hammerheads have been known to attack people in the water.

Rays and Skates

With winglike fins, rays and skates look very different from sharks. However, these cartilaginous fish are really flattened sharks adapted to life on the seabed. There are obvious differences between rays and sharks. For example, rays have flattened bodies with huge, winglike pectoral fins. Rays swim using wavelike motions made by these fins, while sharks swim mostly by the action of their tails. Another difference is that rays have mouths on the undersides of their bodies, with flattened teeth. This allows them to suck up food from the seabed.

Rays and skates do not draw in water through the mouth to breathe because this would block their gills with mud from the seabed. Instead, they have a hole called a spiracle on the top of the head. Water enters the spiracle and then passes over the gills and out through the gill slits.

The tails of rays and skates are designed for protection. Many species have a stinger at the base of the tail that they use to inject a painful poison into an attacker.

▲ The manta or devil ray has two ear-like fins extending forward from the front of the head. This one has remoras attached to its underside, hitching a ride.

Amazing facts

- The largest ray is the manta or devil ray, which measures 23 feet (7 meters) across. It is a harmless filter feeder.

- The torpedo ray has two large organs that contain 1 million electricity-producing cells. They can deliver a 1000-watt shock—enough to stun a human.

▲ The mouth and gill slits of the ray are found on the underside. Rays crush food with their teeth.

Differences between rays and skates

Rays and skates look similar, but they vary in their method of reproduction. Rays give birth to live young while skates lay eggs. There are also a few differences in their appearance. Skates have very thin bodies, tails without tail spines, and up to two dorsal fins at the tip of the tail. Rays usually have a tail spine as well as up to two dorsal fins closer to the body. Finally, male skates often have enlarged, raised scales on the edges of their bodies that they use to grasp females.

Electric weapons

Some species of skates and rays have electricity-producing organs. The electric rays have paired organs located on either side of the head, behind the eyes, with which they can shock and stun their prey. In the skate, these organs are located near the tail. However, the skate can produce only weak electrical fields that are not capable of stunning prey. Researchers believe that the skate's electricity-producing organs are used for communication and to find a mate.

Classification key

CLASS	Chondrichthyes
SUBCLASS	**Elasmobranchii**
ORDERS	3
FAMILIES	13
SPECIES	about 450

◀ Rays may form large schools of several hundred fish.

Bony Fish

The majority of fish have skeletons made of bone. These fish live in virtually every watery habitat. They also vary incredibly in shape. Flat fish, for example, live on the seabed. Some bony fish have amazing shapes for camouflage and look nothing like fish.

Amazing facts

- A type of puffers called fugu is a delicacy in Japan. The fish has to be prepared by special chefs because its skin and internal organs contain a poison that could kill the people eating it.

- About 99 percent of fish die in their first ten months of life.

- As few as one in a million fish live to become adults. Most are eaten while they are still at the egg stage.

▲ These yellow-tailed snappers swim together in a school. This is safer than living alone.

Two classes

There are two classes of bony fish. The more primitive fish are found in the class Sarcopterygii. This class includes coelacanths and lungfish—fish that have fleshy fins. The ray-finned fish of the class Actinopterygii have fins that consist of a web of skin supported by a ray, or spine. Each ray is moved by a set of muscles, making the fin very flexible. This class is large and includes fish such as gars, sturgeons, and bowfins, as well as the very large group of fish known as the teleosts.

The puffers is a spiny-rayed fish found on coral reefs. When threatened, the puffers inflates its body.

Bony skeleton

Along with an internal skeleton made of bone, most bony fish have a covering of scales made of very thin layers of bone. The overlapping scales are covered by a layer of mucus. Catfish have large, bony plates, or scutes, that form armor plating over the body. However, some fish have no scales at all. Most bony fish have two sets of paired fins, but some have only one set of paired fins, and some eels have no paired fins.

Bony fish features

Bony fish have swim bladders. Usually it is a small, round sac filled with air lying beneath the backbone. A few bony fish have swim bladders formed from a pouch off the stomach, and in some fish, this forms a lung.

Bony fish breathe using gills supported by bony arches. The gills are covered by a gill cover, called an operculum. To pass water over their gills, bony fish open their mouths and lower the floor of the mouth. Water rushes in and the fish closes its mouth. They then raise the floor of the mouth to push the water over the gills and back to the outside. Unlike many sharks, bony fish do not have to move to breathe.

Bony fish lay a large number of small eggs that are fertilized in the water, and most do not look after their eggs or their young.

Classification key

CLASSES	2 (Sarcopterygii and Actinopterygii)
ORDERS	46
FAMILIES	437
SPECIES	in excess of 24,000

▶ The goliath grouper is one of the largest bony fish. It can grow up to 8 feet (2.5 meters) long.

Fleshy-finned Fish

In 1938 a fisher off the coast of South Africa hauled up a weird-looking fish. The fish was just under 6.5 feet (2 meters) long and had large, blueish scales. The fish was decayed, so the fisher had it skinned, stuffed, and mounted as a curiosity. A local zoologist later identified the fish as a coelacanth, a lobe-fin fish thought to have been extinct since the time of the dinosaurs. The coelacanth and the lungfish are the only examples that remain of the primitive fleshy-finned fish.

The fleshy-finned fish have a bony skeleton and fleshy fins. The base of each pectoral fin is enlarged by muscles attached to the skeleton. These fins are used for swimming or for pushing themselves along on the seabed. Lungfish use the fins to move on land. It is easy to imagine how these muscular front fins could have evolved into limbs for movement on land.

Amazing facts

- A new species of coelacanth was discovered in Indonesia in 1990, but very little is known about it.
- The word *coelacanth* means "hollow spine."
- Some studies suggest that the Australian lungfish has not changed over the last 100 million years.

Classification key

CLASS	Sarcopterygii
ORDERS	3
FAMILIES	4
SPECIES	8

▼ The Australian lungfish has a heavy body with long pectoral fins. This lungfish does not make burrows.

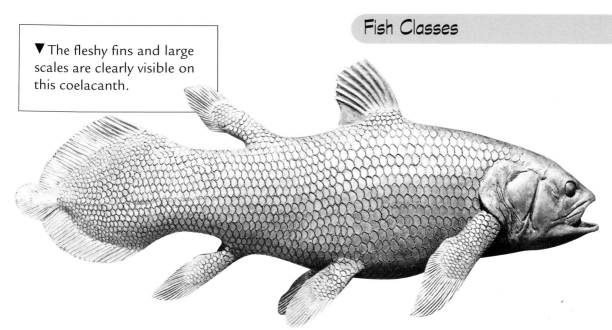

▼ The fleshy fins and large scales are clearly visible on this coelacanth.

The coelacanth

The coelacanth is a deepwater fish that lives at depths of up to 2,300 feet (700 meters). It is a big fish covered by large scales. The coelacanth uses its pectoral fins to wiggle into crevices to catch fish. A hinge at the back of the skull allows the coelacanth to open its mouth very wide.

▲ During the dry season, the African lungfish burrows into the mud and makes a cocoon around its body.

Lungfish

There are six lungfish species that are found in lakes or rivers in Australia, South America, and Africa. The largest, the Australian lungfish, has a heavy body and a swim bladder that acts as a lung. It can use both lungs and gills. This means it can breathe in and out of water. African and South American lungfish are more eel-like, and their paired fins are long and threadlike. When the heat in South America dries up the water supply, lungfish dig into the mud and remain there until it rains. African lungfish dig mud holes, but they also surround themselves with a substance that is produced by their body. As the water disappears, this substance gets drier and forms a kind of leathery cocoon that encases the fish. Lungfish remain dormant until the rains come to release them from their cocoons.

Primitive Ray-finned Fish

The primitive ray-finned fish are unusual because they have skeletons that are partly bone and partly cartilage. They have gills and lungs, just like the coelacanths and lungfish, although most just use their gills. There are four groups of primitive ray-finned fish: sturgeons and paddlefish; gars; bichirs; and bowfins. Ray-finned fish are generally large, and most are found in freshwater. However, a few live in both salt water and freshwater.

▼ Sturgeon are among the most endangered river fish because humans eat their eggs. They have sharklike bodies and plates instead of scales.

Classification key

CLASS	Actinopterygii
ORDERS	**Acipenseriformes (sturgeon and paddlefish), Amiiformes (bowfins), Lepisosteiformes (gars), Polypteriformes (bichirs)**
FAMILIES	5
SPECIES	43

Sturgeons and paddlefish

The sturgeon, the largest of the freshwater fish, weighs about 606 pounds (275 kilograms). It has a body like a shark, with a long, flat snout and five rows of bony plates rather than scales. The sturgeon's skeleton is partly cartilaginous. The paddlefish has a long, paddle-shaped snout that may be used to help it sense its surroundings. Paddlefish are filter feeders. They filter the water for food as it passes through their gills.

► The body of the bichir is covered in large scales. It can breathe air by using its swim bladder like a lung.

Gars

The gar is a large, predatory fish found in the rivers of North America. Its jaw is covered in small, sharp teeth. It will wait for its prey by hanging motionless in the water. Then it will jump out to catch its prey

Amazing facts

- Sturgeon, the largest freshwater fish, grow up to 26 feet (8 meters) long.
- At 1.65 tons, the Russian sturgeon is the heaviest kind of sturgeon.
- The European sturgeon may travel more than 620 miles (1,000 kilometers) from the sea to its river breeding grounds.

Bichirs

The bichir is a bottom-dwelling fish found in the Nile and in the rivers of west Africa. Bichirs have long bodies, stubby fins, and a row of tiny fins along their backs that they can raise or lower like little sails. They can breathe air and crawl along river beds using their pectoral fins.

Bowfins

The bowfin is smaller than the other primitive ray-finned fish. It has a large mouth with many sharp teeth. There are no scales on its head. The dorsal fin extends more than half the length of the back, and the tail is round in shape. The bowfin is a predatory fish that feeds on small fish.

▼ The paddlefish is named after the amazing spine that sticks out beyond its head. Its large mouth swallows water that is filtered for food.

Eels, Tarpons, and Halosaurs

The eel looks like a snake without scales. The fins are small, and in many species the paired fins are absent. Most eels have a ribbon-shaped fin that runs along the back, around the tail, and under the body.

Surprisingly, eels are classified together with two very different groups of fish: the tarpons and halosaurs. Although these fish look nothing like each other, they are grouped together in one large superorder because they have similar life cycles. These fish produce eggs that develop into long, thin, transparent larvae. Their larvae spend several years drifting in ocean currents as part of the plankton.

The European eel

The European eel has an unusual life cycle. Between the ages of four and eighteen years, it lives in freshwater rivers and lakes. Then it travels down rivers to the Atlantic Ocean, slithering across land if necessary. It switches to living in salt water. It swims thousands of miles across the Atlantic to the Sargasso Sea. The eels gather deep in the middle of the ocean, where they lay their eggs and then die. The eggs hatch into microscopic larvae that spend three years living among the plankton, gradually moving back across the ocean. By the time the elvers, or young eels, are four years old, they are ready to move back to freshwater. They swim up rivers, where they spend the next fourteen years.

▼ Eels, such as this European eel, have a single fin running down the back, around the tail, and along the underside.

Tarpons and halosaurs

The tarpon is a large predatory fish. The last ray of its dorsal fin is formed into a long thread, and its body is covered in huge scales. The tarpon's large mouth points upward. The halosaur is a deep-sea fish, and very little is known about it.

Deep-sea relatives

A number of the members of this superorder are deep-sea fish that live at depths of up to 6,500 feet (2,000 meters). In the deep there is little food, and these fish have to eat whatever comes along. The swallower and gulper eels look like eels have huge mouths and stomachs that can expand to cope with large prey.

▲ The leptocephalus larva of the eel is shaped like a willow leaf, an ideal shape for drifting in plankton.

Classification key

CLASS	Actinopterygii
SUPERORDER	**Elopomorpha**
ORDERS	5—Elopiformes, Albuliformes, Notacanthiformes, Anguilliformes, Saccopharyngiformes
FAMILIES	24
SPECIES	800

▶ The brightly colored, aggressive moray eel hides itself in holes in the rocks and attacks passing fish.

Amazing facts

- The European eel makes a journey of more than 3,600 miles (6,000 kilometers) from its river of birth to the Sargasso Sea.

- Young eels, known as leptocephalus larvae, look so different from the adults that scientists who first discovered them thought they were a completely different species.

Herring and Anchovies

Herring are mostly small fish with silvery, streamlined bodies. They travel together in large schools and make up an important part of the ocean food chain. Herring feed on plankton. They are hunted by predatory fish, birds, dolphins, and whales.

▲ A single school of anchovies can contain as many as 100,000 fish.

Herring relatives

Along with the various herring species, this superorder also contains pilchards and anchovies. These fish are very similar in shape to herring, but are much smaller. Anchovies and herring have swim bladders linked to their inner ears, and this arrangement is believed to improve their hearing. Good hearing is essential for keeping the schools of fish together, especially when the school is under attack from predators.

Filter feeding

Herring feed on zooplankton—tiny animals that are found in the surface waters of the oceans. It is too dangerous for herring to feed at the surface during the day because predators would spot the schools. During daylight the herring stay in the safety of the deeper dark water. They venture to the surface only at night when there is less chance of being seen. Herring swim along with their mouths open, filtering the plankton from the water as it passes through their gills. Young herring feed on plant plankton, and as they grow they start to eat larger organisms. Adult herring feed on crustaceans, fish eggs, and the larvae of fish and mollusks found among plankton.

▲ Herring have silvery bodies. They may live for as long as 20 years.

Swirling schools

Herring are a favorite food of many of the ocean hunters. It is safer to be in a school than to swim alone, so herring come together in large numbers. When a school is under attack from predators such as dolphins, marlin, or tuna, the fish swim close together to form a dense, swirling ball that twists and turns as one. This is to confuse the predator and make it difficult for individual fish to be caught and eaten. The predators try to break up the school and cause the fish to scatter.

Classification key

CLASS	Actinopterygii
SUPERORDER	Clupeimorpha
ORDER	**Clupeiformes (herring and anchovy)**
FAMILIES	5
SPECIES	357

▼ Anchovies are food for a variety of marine animals, including seals, predatory fish, and seabirds.

Carp, Catfish, and Piranhas

Carp and their relatives are the most common of the freshwater fish. They are found in ponds, rivers, and lakes around the world. There are four orders within the superorder of Ostariophysi. They include catfish, carp and minnows, characins, and milkfish. The characins include the notorious piranha as well as well-known fish such as the tetras and tiger barbs that are frequently kept in tropical aquariums.

Classification key

CLASS	Actinopterygii
SUPERORDER	**Ostariophysi**
ORDERS	5—Gonorynchiformes (milkfish), Cypriniformes (carp and minnows), Characiformes (characins), Gymnotiformes (electric fish), and Siluriformes (catfish)
FAMILIES	62
SPECIES	approximately 6,500

Acute senses

These fish have a particularly well-developed sense of hearing. This is due to uniquely modified vertebrae in the spine. These bones transmit sounds from the swim bladder to the inner ear, which magnifies the sound. This modified spine is called the Weberian apparatus.

Catfish and their relatives are bottom-dwelling fish that spend their lives on the beds of ponds, lakes, and rivers. They rely on whiskerlike barbels around the mouth to find food in the dark. The barbels are covered in taste buds. They give the catfish an excellent sense of touch and taste.

▼ King carp are found in lakes and slow-flowing rivers. They feed by sucking up invertebrates and plants from the mud.

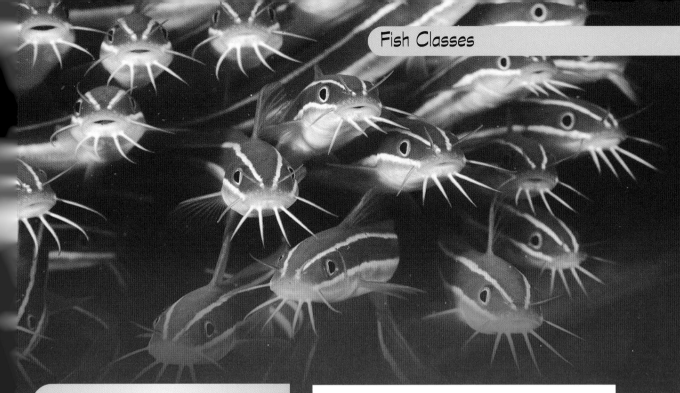

Amazing facts

- The electric eel can produce a bolt of electricity of up to 600 volts, which is powerful enough to kill large fish and even knock a person off his or her feet.
- The wels is one of the largest freshwater fish. The heaviest one caught in Russia weighed 730 pounds (330 kilograms).

▲ The catfish has two long barbels attached to its upper lip and a cluster of smaller barbels on its lower lip.

Piranhas

Piranhas live in the rivers of South America, and most eat fruit that falls into the water. However, the red piranha is a deadly predator with a blunt face and a lower jaw that is longer than its upper jaw. Red piranhas hunt in schools, usually attacking other fish. However, they will eat larger animals that fall into the river, including sloths and deer.

Electric eel

The electric eel's name seems to place it in another group, but it still belongs to this superorder. Electric eels have poor eyesight and rely on their electricity-producing organ to find their way around. They kill their prey with strong electric shocks.

▲ Red piranhas have small teeth on both jaws. The upper and lower teeth fit together perfectly when the fish closes its jaws. This allows the red piranha to rip off lumps of flesh.

Salmon

There are more than 300 species of salmon and their relatives. This group contains pike, char, smelt, and grayling as well as salmon and trout. Most of these fish are predators that chase their prey through the water or wait in the shadows for prey to pass by.

Powerful swimmers

These fish are characterized by long, muscular, tapering bodies. Most of the fins are small except for the tail fin, which is large and powerful enough to propel the fish through the water at great speeds. Many have a small fin near the base of the tail, called the adipose fin. They either have small scales or no scales at all.

Amazing facts

- Grayling are particularly sensitive to pollution. Their presence in a river indicates that the water is clean.
- The unusual searsid emits a liquid that glows an eerie green in the water. This may distract predators so the fish can escape.
- The eulachon is nicknamed the candle fish because it is so oily that its flesh would burn like a candle.

▲ The powerful tail of the salmon helps it to leap up waterfalls and rapids on the journey to its spawning grounds.

▲ In favorable conditions, millions of salmon swim up the river together over a period of just a few weeks.

Classification key

CLASS	Actinopterygii
SUPERORDER	**Protacanthopterygii**
ORDERS	3—Esociformes (pike), Osmeriformes (smelts), and Salmoniformes (salmon, trout, and grayling)
FAMILIES	16
SPECIES	312

Saltwater and freshwater

This group of fish contains both freshwater and saltwater species. Pike, for example, are found in lakes and rivers. Salmon is an unusual fish because at different stages of its life it lives in either freshwater or salt water. Salmon are born in freshwater, but they move to the ocean to mature. After several years, they return to freshwater to breed. Trout can spend their whole lives in freshwater, but the sea trout can migrate between freshwater and salt water.

Fish farming

Today, salmon and trout are farmed. Salmon are kept in large ocean pens until they are large enough for harvesting. Trout are often raised in pens and then released into lakes for fishers to catch and throw back into the water.

▶ Pike lurk among waterweeds, waiting for their prey to come close. Their large mouths allow them to swallow prey half their own size.

The Sockeye Salmon

The sockeye salmon is a large fish found in the northern part of the Pacific Ocean. Just like all salmon, the sockeye spends its adult life at sea before returning to freshwater to breed. However, this species is restricted to rivers located along lakes because the larval fish spend time growing in lake waters.

▲ Breeding adult sockeye salmon have bright red bodies. The male has a hooked jaw and a humped back.

Life begins

Sockeye salmon begin life in freshwater streams during the autumn. Female salmon lay their eggs in gravel nests, called redds, that they have dug in the streambed. Each female lays about 4,000 bright pink eggs. After the eggs have been fertilized by the male, she covers them with gravel for protection. Then the adult salmon die, exhausted from their journey and from digging and guarding their redds.

In spring, the eggs hatch into small larval fish, called alevin, that still have their yolk sacs attached. Alevin usually stay in the redds for about a week until they absorb their yolk sacs. Then they are called fry. The fry swim downstream to a lake where they stay for between one and three years, feeding on plankton and insect larvae. The fry grow quickly. Finally, they migrate to the ocean. Young salmon that are ready to enter the ocean are called smolts.

▶ In some rivers there are so many sockeye salmon that the water looks red.

Dangerous journey

Smolts face many hazards on their journey to the sea, including predators, hydroelectric dams, and pollution. Those that survive the journey enter the sea, where they feed and grow until they become adult salmon. At full size, salmon are just under 3 feet (1 meter) long and weigh up to 15 pounds (7 kilograms). While at sea they are sleek and silvery in color.

▲ Pink salmon eggs settle in the gravel bed and are covered by the female.

Breeding

When salmon are four years old, they return to the rivers where they were born in order to breed. They swim for hundreds of miles up rivers to the spawning ground. They face the same hazards on the return journey as they faced on the way to the sea. Many adults die on the way. During this time, the salmon's appearance changes. The head turns blue-green, and the body becomes bright red. The male salmon develop a hooked jaw and a humped back.

Amazing facts

- In some rivers, millions of salmon swim up the river over a short period of time. This spectacle has become a popular tourist attraction in Washington state and in Canada.

- Some salmon make a final journey of up to 1,500 miles (2,500 kilometers) from the ocean to the spawning ground.

- Sockeye salmon that stay in lakes and never go to sea are called kokanee. These sockeyes live in freshwater and die after spawning. They are very similar to the sea-going sockeye, but they are generally much smaller.

Classification key

CLASS	Actinopterygii
SUPERORDER	Protacanthopterygii
GENUS	*Oncorhynchus*
SPECIES	***nerka***

Anglers, Cod, and Toadfish

▲ This Australian anglerfish stays hidden. Its white, horseshoe-shaped lure attracts prey.

The group of anglers, cod, and toadfish contains fish of varied appearances. The cod looks like a typical fish, but the anglerfish and toadfish are among some of the strangest-looking fish in the sea.

Bizarre appearance

Most anglerfish and toadfish are bottom dwellers. They use stealth and camouflage to catch their prey. Some look like pieces of seaweed, while others resemble stones or the seabed. They all have large mouths to suck in their prey. The anglerfish is named after its dorsal spine, which ends in a lure that looks like a fishing rod. The fish lies perfectly still on the seabed and jiggles its spine to move the lure and attract fish. Its mouth can open and shut so quickly that the prey appears to vanish. Anglerfish are found in the deepest parts of the ocean, where they live in cold and dark water. They have lures containing bacteria that produce light. Frogfish, a type of anglerfish, are found on coral reefs. They are small and brightly colored. They look more like coral than fish. Like the anglerfish, they use lures to attract their prey.

Classification key

CLASS	Actinopterygii
SUPERORDER	**Protacanthopterygii**
ORDERS	5
FAMILIES	37
SPECIES	approximately 1,200

▲ Cod have a typical fish shape, with a streamlined body. They feed near the seabed.

Amazing facts

- A female cod lays as many as nine million eggs each year.
- The male oyster toadfish produces a sound like a foghorn that may attract females to a nesting site.
- About 100 years ago, fishermen sometimes caught cod that weighed up to 200 pounds (90 kilograms). However, today anything over 30 pounds (15 kilograms) is rare.

Cod and whiting

There are about 500 cod species, including Atlantic cod, haddock, and whiting. These fish have long, narrow bodies with a dorsal fin that is divided up into several sections. Their bodies are covered in small scales. Most have a single barbel under the chin. Cod are found in large schools. They are predatory fish that hunt smaller fish such as herring. They tend to feed in deep water at about 1,900 feet (600 meters), just above the seabed.

Cod spawn in shallow water. The female lays her eggs near or on the seabed, where they are fertilized by the male. Then the eggs float to the surface and the larvae hatch and drift with the plankton. The cod lays many more eggs than most other species. This is necessary because so few of the eggs will hatch and even fewer of the larvae will survive.

Cod species are caught in large amounts by fishers, especially in the Atlantic Ocean. Unfortunately, too many have been caught and the numbers of some species, such as the Atlantic cod, are dangerously low.

▶ The outline of the frogfish resembles pieces of coral. This provides excellent camouflage in a coral reef.

49

Spiny-rayed Fish

Spiny-rayed fish make up more than half of all fish. This is a varied group, ranging in size, body shape, and color. The largest are more than 25 feet (8 meters) long while the smallest is 0.4 inches (1 centimeter) long.

Stiff, bony spines

The name of this group comes from the stiff, bony spines these fish have in their dorsal fins. In some, the spine is just in front of the dorsal fin. However, a few fish lack the spines and some lack the dorsal fin completely. There are five main groups within the spiny-rayed fish: lionfish, flying fish, perch, triggerfish, and flatfish.

Lionfish and flying fish

There are more than 1,200 species of lionfish, dories, and oarfish. The lionfish, with its fan-shaped fins, spines, and striped body, is a common sight on coral reefs. Another group of unusual-looking fish contains the flying fish, grunions, and sea horse. The flying fish can glide over the surface of the ocean on outstretched fins. It may trail the end of its tail in the water. The tail acts a bit like a propeller, pushing the fish forward. Grunions wiggle onto sandy beaches where they mate and lay their eggs. The sea horse is named after its horse-shaped head. Its body is covered in bony plates, and it swims upright, pushed along by tiny fins.

▶ Lionfish have fins tipped with sharp spines that can inject poison into the skin of a predator.

▲ The barracuda has a streamlined shape with a long, thin body, stiff fins, and a crescent-shaped tail fin.

Amazing facts

- The dwarf goby is just under 0.4 inches (1 centimeter) long, but its relative, the oarfish, is more than 25 feet (8 meters) in length.
- The flying fish can glide over the water for more than 650 feet (200 meters).
- The mudskipper spends most of its time out of water and breathes through its skin.

Perch, triggerfish, and flatfish

Perch and its relatives (about 9,500 species) all have spiny dorsal fins. In many species the fin is long and extends along the back as far as the tail. This group ranges dramatically in size and includes groupers, cichlids, mudskippers, parrot fish, barracudas, and marlin.

Triggerfish vary in shape. Some species are box-shaped, but others are round. Triggerfish have small mouths and backbone with fewer vertebrae than other fish. Examples include the box fish, porcupine fish, triggerfish, and ocean sunfish.

Flatfish, such as plaice, flounder, and halibut, live on the seabed. They always lie on one side with both eyes pointing upward.

Classification key

CLASS	Actinopterygii
SUPERORDER	**Acanthopterygii**
ORDERS	14
FAMILIES	approximately 250
SPECIES	approximately 13,500

▶ This pink anemone fish lives among the stinging tentacles of the sea anemone where it is safe from predators. Its body produces a substance that protects it from the stings.

Bizarre shapes

There are some unusually shaped fish among the spiny-rayed fish. Some have bodies that are shaped to blend in with the background. Some are huge and do not appear to be streamlined. Others undergo a complete transformation in shape as they grow older.

Amazing facts

- The Atlantic halibut is the world's largest flatfish. It can weigh up to 650 pounds (300 kilograms).
- The stonefish has poisonous dorsal spines. Many people have died after stepping on a stonefish in shallow water.
- The sunfish is the heaviest of the bony fish, weighing up to 2 tons.

Camouflage

Sea horses and weedy sea dragons are camouflaged in such a way that they are difficult to spot among seaweed. The weedy sea dragon has leaflike flaps that disguise the outline of its body. The stonefish also uses camouflage to hide on the seabed as it lies in wait for prey to pass by. Its body is colored to look like pieces of rock.

▲ The weedy sea dragon is a master of camouflage. It lives among seaweed. The many leafy flaps sticking out of its body make it almost invisible to predators.

▲ Groupers are heavy, slow-moving fish with wide mouths and lots of teeth.

The giants

There are some huge spiny-rayed fish. The giant grouper is larger than a human. This fish grows very slowly, which means that the largest individuals are many years old. Another odd-looking giant is the ocean sunfish. Its body is round and flat like a huge dinner plate. The opah, or moonfish, has an oval-shaped body that is up to 7 feet (2 meters) long. Although the moonfish is large, its fins slip easily through water as it chases smaller fish. Another giant is the oarfish. This rare fish looks like a huge, silvery ribbon edged with a single red fin.

The flatfish

The larvae of flatfish live in plankton for about six weeks and then they begin an amazing transformation. Imagine a fish lying on its side, with one of the eyes pointing down. As a flatfish develops, this eye moves across the head so that it comes to lie on the upper side next to the other eye. The body becomes flatter. The upper side is darker and speckled so that the fish is camouflaged when lying on the seabed. This side can change color to blend in with the background. Most flatfish feed on invertebrates that live on the seabed. However, the halibut is an active predator that chases other fish.

▶ This plaice is lying on its left-hand side. Both of its eyes lie on the right-hand side that faces up from the seabed.

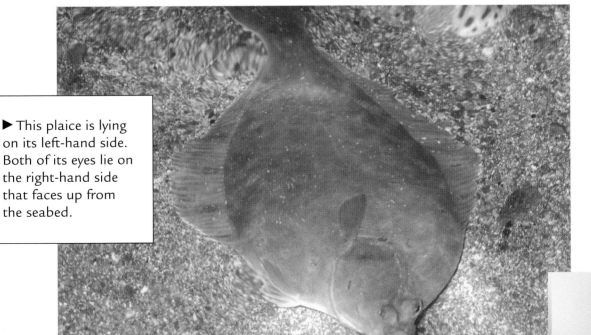

Fish Under Threat

Fish tend to be overlooked when people think of animals in danger. Yet all around the world, fish are under threat. Many people who eat Atlantic cod do not realize that they are eating an endangered animal.

The biggest threat to fish comes from overfishing. Whitefish such as cod are being fished at a level that cannot be sustained. Fishers prefer to catch large fish, but these are the breeding fish. As the larger fish disappear, the fishers have to catch the smaller, younger fish. Young fish must be able to reach a certain age and size in order to breed. If too many young fish are caught, then too few will survive to breed. In the North Sea, it is likely that the fishing of many species will have to be drastically cut or even stopped if the fish are to survive. In the past, North Sea herring stocks were so low that all fishing had to be stopped for ten years. Fish are overfished in rivers and lakes, too.

Sharks are caught for their fins, which are used in shark fin soup, a Chinese delicacy. As a result, shark numbers have fallen rapidly. The process for getting shark fins is cruel and wasteful. The sharks are caught, their fins sliced off, and then they are thrown back into the water to drown or be eaten by other animals.

▼ When sharks are caught, their fins are removed and they are thrown back into the water to die.

▲ Each year, trawlers catch millions of tons of fish such as this redfish. On factory ships, the fish are made ready for market.

Polluted water

Around the world, raw sewage, industrial waste, and garbage are dumped into rivers, estuaries, and oceans. Fertilizers and pesticides run off agricultural land into water. These pollutants harm aquatic organisms, including fish.

Habitat loss

Mangrove swamps are important fish nurseries. Many fish species lay their eggs in the shallow waters of coastal mangrove swamps. The young fish live in this habitat before swimming out to sea. However, many mangroves are being cleared to make way for tourist developments and new ports. This important habitat is slowly being destroyed.

Amazing facts

- Over the last 50 years, the populations of predatory fish such as tuna, marlin, and great white sharks, have fallen by 90 percent.
- Sea horses are under threat because they are collected, dried, and used in traditional medicines. Some are sold as souvenirs.
- Worldwide, fishing fleets kill an estimated 100 million sharks a year. If nothing is done, some species could become extinct within 50 to 100 years.

Fish as pets

Many people keep tropical fish as pets. Most of the common species such as guppies and neon tetras are bred in captivity. However, fish that live in saltwater aquariums can be difficult to keep and they do not breed well. These fish are often collected from coral reefs and transported to Europe and North America, where they are sold in pet shops.

▶ Colorful tropical fish are trapped in cages on the seabed and then flown around the world, where they end up in tropical fish tanks as pets.

Protecting Fish

There are many ways in which fish stocks around the world are being protected. The most important places to protect are the spawning grounds of the fish. These are the places where the fish lay their eggs. Banning all fishing in such areas is a good way to protect the spawning grounds. Some fish are already being protected. The spawning grounds of the Atlantic cod in the North Sea are protected. Off the coast of Belize, the Nassau grouper has been given protection and is off-limits to fishers.

Amazing facts

- Since 1993 shark finning has been banned in the Atlantic and in the Gulf of Mexico. The ban was extended to the Pacific in 2002.
- In 2002 the European Union banned shark finning in its waters.
- The European Union has regulations that prevent fishers from using nets with a small mesh. During the 1980s the mesh size of nets was increased. This means that the smaller, younger fish can escape.

Quotas

Quotas, or allowances, can control the quantity of fish taken from the ocean. The United States federal government regulates the quantity of fish that can be fished in its waters. Other countries have similar restrictions. It is difficult, however, to control the fishing that takes place in international waters—the open seas outside the territorial waters of any nation. New global regulations may be needed to protect some species such as tuna, marlin, and the larger sharks.

▶ Many of the world's coral reefs have been given protection, and this should help to conserve the fish.

◀ It is illegal for fishers or divers to catch the Nassau grouper.

New mangroves

Some countries have realized that their mangrove swamps are important. They have found that clearing the swamps has led to a decline in their fish stocks. Fish is the main source of protein in the diet for many people living along tropical coastlines and on islands. So maintaining healthy fish stocks is essential. Today, some mangroves are being replanted. Mangroves grow quickly, so it will not be long before these new mangroves can act as valuable fish nurseries.

Controlling fish trade

Education is important in the battle to protect our fish. Local people should know the value of their coastal waters and their fish stocks. They learn ways to conserve them. In some places, people are breeding tropical fish in captivity for the pet trade so that fish do not have to be taken from the wild. It is also important that people who have tropical aquariums ask questions about the origins of the fish that they buy.

▼ In some places, divers can get close to sharks and rays by feeding them. This is a popular tourist activity. Local people are more likely to protect the sharks because the tourists bring money into the area.

Classification

Scientists know of about two million different kinds of animals. With so many species, it is important that they be classified into groups so that they can be described more accurately. The groups show how living organisms are related through evolution and where they belong in the natural world. A scientist identifies an animal by looking at features such as the number of legs or the type of teeth. Animals that share the same characteristics belong to the same species. Scientists place species with similar characteristics in the same genus. The genera are grouped together in families, which in turn are grouped into orders, and orders are grouped into classes. Classes are grouped together in phyla and finally, phyla are grouped into kingdoms. Kingdoms are the largest groups. There are five kingdoms: monerans (bacteria), protists (single-celled organisms), fungi, plants, and animals.

Naming an animal

Each species has a unique Latin name that consists of two words. The first word is the name of the genus to which the organism belongs. The second is the name of its species. For example, the Latin name of the sockeye salmon is *Oncorhynchos nerka* and the pink salmon is *Oncorhynchos gorbuscha*. This tells us that these animals are grouped in the same genus but are different species. Many animals have common names that vary from one part of the world to another. For example, the sockeye salmon is also called the red salmon and the blue back. Sometimes there are very small differences between individuals in the same species. So there is an extra division called a subspecies. To show that an animal belongs to a subspecies, another name is added to the end of the Latin name.

▲ During the breeding season, sockeye salmon undergo a color change from silvery blue to red. These colors give rise to the salmon's other names of red salmon and blueback.

This table shows how a great white shark is classified.

Classification	Example: great white shark	Features
Kingdom	Animalia	Sharks belong to the kingdom Animalia because they have many cells, need to eat food, and are formed from a fertilized egg.
Phylum	Chordata	An animal from the phylum Chordata has a strengthening rod called a notochord running down its back and gill pouches. In the subphylum Vertebrata, the notochord is replaced by a backbone.
Class	Chondrichthyes	Sharks have a cartilaginous skeleton, no swim bladders, and a skin that is covered in tiny scales called denticles.
Subclass	Elasmobranchii	Elasmobranchs have five to seven gill slits on each side of the head and teeth that are replaced throughout life.
Order	Lamniformes	Sharks of this order have two dorsal fins, no spines, no nictitating membrane over the eye, and a mouth that ends behind the eyes.
Family	Lamnidae (mackerel sharks)	The mackerel sharks have a sharply pointed snout, large mouth, and crescent-shaped tail fin. They also have specialized blood circulation around the muscles to retain heat.
Genus	*Carcharodon*	A feature of this genus is jagged teeth.
Species	*carcharias*	A species is a grouping of individuals that interbreed successfully. The great white shark's species name is *carcharias*.

Fish Evolution

The first fish appeared about 500 million years ago. They were ostracoderms—jawless fish covered in bony scales. They did not have any paired fins and were less than 12 inches (30 centimeters) long. They moved along the bottom of seas and lakes, where they hunted mostly arthropods. Their gills were large and were used for breathing and filtering food from the water. There were many types of jawless fish, but most died out about 350 million years ago. Today, the only survivors are lampreys and hagfish.

▲ An ancestor of this colorful triggerfish is a spiny shark, called an acanthodian, that lived 400 million years ago.

The first fish with jaws, the acanthodians or spiny sharks, appeared about 440 to 450 million years ago. They became extinct about 250 million years ago. Acanthodians were generally small, sharklike fish. Experts believe that the acanthodians and modern bony fish are related and that either the acanthodians gave rise to the modern bony fish or that they share a common ancestor.

The placoderms, another group of jawed fish, appeared about 395 million years ago. Placoderms were typically small, flattened bottom dwellers with bony skeletons. They became extinct about 345 million years ago. Cartilaginous fish appeared about 370 million years ago and may be descended from the placoderms. Scientists believe that the cartilaginous skeleton developed from the bony skeleton. It is difficult to find fossil remains of the earliest sharks because their cartilaginous skeletons have not survived. However, scientists have used millions of scales and teeth to identify about 3,000 different shark species.

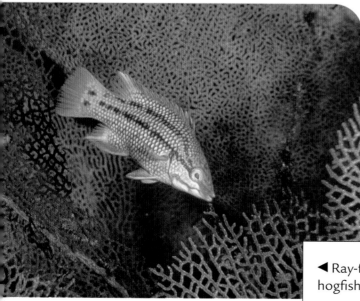

◀ Ray-finned fish, such as this Mexican hogfish, first appeared 260 million years ago.

About 250 million years ago, there was a mass extinction. There was a major change in the global environment and more than 99 percent of all marine species, including many types of sharks, were wiped out. However, a few survived. One of these gave rise to modern sharks.

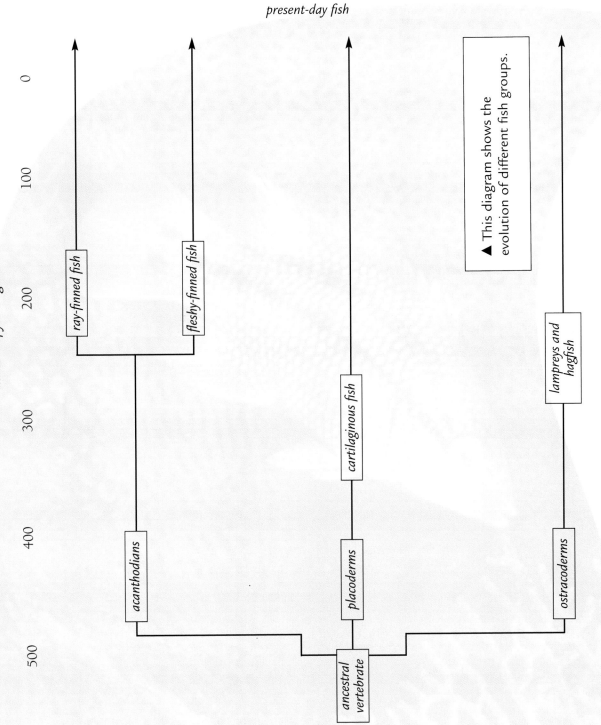

present-day fish

millions of years ago

0

100

200

300

400

500

ray-finned fish

fleshy-finned fish

cartilaginous fish

lampreys and hagfish

acanthodians

placoderms

ostracoderms

ancestral vertebrate

▲ This diagram shows the evolution of different fish groups.

Glossary

adapt change in order to cope with the environment

aquatic living in water

barbel whiskerlike structure around mouth of fish that is covered in sensory cells

binocular vision having two eyes close together so that a three-dimensional image is produced. This helps when judging distances

blood vessel tube that transports blood around an animal's body

breed mate and produce young

buoyant able to float

camouflage coloring that blends with the background, making an animal difficult to see

cartilage flexible structural material found in the bodies of animals. It is found in the nose and ears of mammals and in the skeletons of rays and sharks.

characteristic feature or quality of an animal, such as having hair or having wings

coral reef ridge near the surface of the sea in a tropical climate that is formed by masses of the skeletons of tiny sea creatures

current flow of water in a particular direction

DNA substance found in the cells of nearly all living organisms that provides information about an organism's makeup

dormant inactive

ectothermic having a body temperature that rises and falls with the outside temperature, often referred to as cold-blooded

embryo very early stage of development in animal life

evolution organism's slow process of change that makes it better suited to live in its environment

evolve change very slowly over a long period of time

extinct no longer in existence; permanently disappeared

fertilize cause a female to produce young through the introduction of male reproductive material

fossil remains, trace, or impression of ancient life preserved in rock

fin thin flap of skin supported by spines found sticking out of a fish's body

gill part of the body that an aquatic animal uses to collect oxygen from water. In fish, the gills are inside the body.

interbreed mate with another animal of the same species

invertebrate animal without a backbone

larva (plural: **larvae**) young animal that looks different from its parents and changes shape as it develops

lure feature of some fish resembling a fishing rod that is used to attract prey

mammal class of vertebrates that feed their young milk, are usually covered in hair, and have a constant body temperature

mate ability of male to fertilize the eggs of a female of the same species

membrane thin, flexible sheet of tissue that covers parts of an organism

migration regular journey made by an animal, often linked to the changes of the seasons

mucus thick, sticky substance

organism any living thing

parasite animal that lives on or in another animal and causes harm to it

plankton group of microscopic plants and animals that live in water

pore tiny hole in the surface of skin through which liquids such as sweat may pass

predator animal that hunts other animals

pressure continuous force exerted on a body from outside, such as the force of water on the body of a fish

prey animal that is killed and eaten by other animals

primitive at an early stage of evolution or development. For example, jawless fish are considered to be primitive because they lack the jaw found in all other fish.

scale small plate covering the body of fish

sensory cell cell that can detect changes in the environment, such as changes in light, smell, heat, movement, or vibration

skeleton bony framework of an animal

sound wave vibration that produces sound

spawn release or deposit eggs

species group of individuals that share many characteristics and can interbreed to produce offspring

streamlined having a slim shape that moves through water as easily as possible

swim bladder air-filled sac that keeps fish afloat when they are not swimming

vertebrate animal that has a backbone

viviparous giving birth to live young

Further Information

Fullick, Ann. *Ecosystems & Environment.* Chicago: Heinemann Library, 2000.

Sachidhanandam, Uma. *Threatened Habitats.* Chicago: Raintree, 2004.

Solway, Andrew. *Killer Fish.* Chicago: Heinemann Library, 2005.

Spilsbury, Louise and Richard Spilsbury. *Classifying Fish.* Chicago: Heinemann Library, 2003.

Spilsbury, Louise and Richard Spilsbury. *The Life Cycle of Fish.* Chicago: Heinemann Library, 2003.

Townsend, John. *Incredible Fish.* Chicago: Raintree, 2005.

Index